T0190667

A Mustang's Tale

THIS EDITION
Editorial Management by Oriel Square
Produced for DK by WonderLab Group LLC
Jennifer Emmett, Erica Green, Kate Hale, *Founders*

Editor Maya Myers; **Photography Editor** Nicole DiMella; **Managing Editor** Rachel Houghton;
Designers Project Design Company; **Researcher** Michelle Harris;
Copy Editor Lori Merritt; **Indexer** Connie Binder; **Proofreader** Susan K. Hom;
Authenticity Reader Dr. Naomi R. Caldwell; **Series Reading Specialist** Dr. Jennifer Albro

First American Edition, 2024
Published in the United States by DK Publishing, a division of Penguin Random House LLC
1745 Broadway, 20th Floor, New York, NY 10019

Copyright © 2024 Dorling Kindersley Limited
24 25 26 27 10 9 8 7 6 5 4 3 2 1
001-342885-Sep/2024

A catalog record for this book is available from the Library of Congress.
HC ISBN: 978-0-5938-4719-0
PB ISBN: 978-0-5938-4718-3

DK books are available at special discounts when purchased in bulk for sales promotions, premiums, fund-raising,
or educational use. For details, contact:
DK Publishing Special Markets, 1745 Broadway, 20th Floor, New York, NY 10019
SpecialSales@dk.com

Printed and bound in China

The publisher would like to thank the following for their kind permission to reproduce their images:
a=above; c=center; b=below; l=left; r=right; t=top; b/g=background
Alamy Stock Photo: franzfoto.com 21b, Lee Rentz 13br, Juergen Sohns 19br; **Comstock:** Masterfile 3;
Dreamstime.com: Bpm1982 18b, David Burke 7bl, 9br, Dejavu Designs 15br, Ken Desloover 10b, 23bl,
Maria Luisa Lopez Estivill 15bc, Corey A Ford 13bl, Alexey Kamenskiy 14b, Elena Lelikova 6b,
Mitchellphotographic 12-13, Thomas Olson 11br, Photoredaktor 10-11, Alexander Pytskiy 16b, Manuel Ribeiro 8-9,
23cla, Septemberrain 11bc, Taiga 5br, 20-21, 22, 23clb, Twildlife 20b, Jorn Vangoidtsenhoven 8b;
Getty Images: John Finney Photography 4b, Moment / Don Cook 23cl, Moment / Marcia Straub 12b,
Moment / Teresa Kopec 1, Photodisc / Bluefootage 18-19, Photodisc / Eastcott Momatiuk 16-17,
The Image Bank / Mark Newman 4-5, 6-7, 23tl; **Getty Images / iStock:** Mari_Art 17b, Mcpuckette 5bc;
naturepl.com: Carol Walker 14-15; **Shutterstock.com:** Ronnie Howard 7bc, Chnkant Samphanthphngs 9bc

Cover images: *Front:* **Dreamstime.com:** Ernest Akayeu (Horse); **Getty Images / iStock:** Elena Borodulina
(Background); *Back:* **Dreamstime.com:** Ernest Akayeu cra, Pavel Naumov clb

All other images © Dorling Kindersley Limited
For more information see: www.dkimages.com

www.dk.com

MIX
Paper | Supporting
responsible forestry
FSC® C018179

This book was made with Forest
Stewardship Council™ certified
paper — one small step in DK's
commitment to a sustainable future.
Learn more at
www.dk.com/uk/information/sustainability

A Mustang's Tale

Angela Modany

A baby mustang is born in the spring.
It is called a foal.

grassland

The foal is born in the grassland.
The grassland is flat.
This is the foal's home.

The foal has
a family.
A family
of mustangs
is called a band.
The foal is part
of the band.

foal

One mustang is the leader of the band. The leader helps to keep the band safe.

band

The mustangs run.
They get hungry.
They stop to eat.
Mustangs eat grass.
Sometimes, they eat
weeds and shrubs.

shrubs

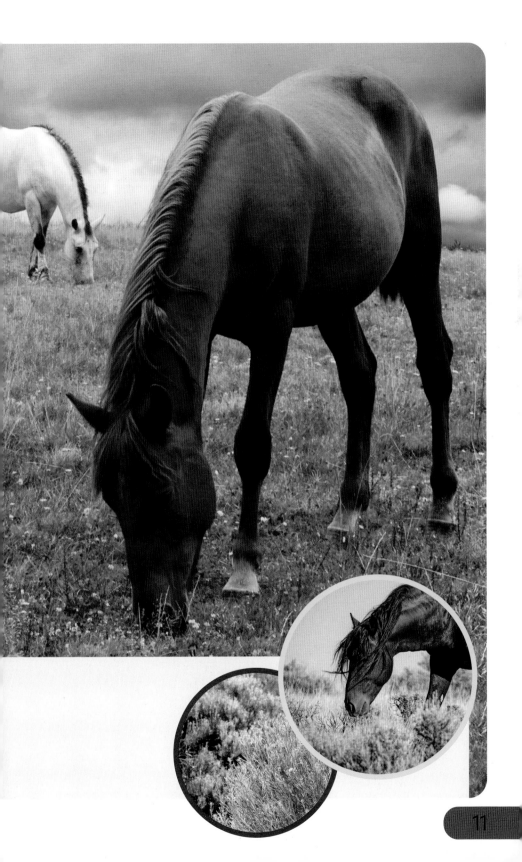

In the winter, it snows.
The snow covers the
grassland.
The mustangs dig
through the snow.
They find grass
to eat.

snow

It is cold
in the winter.
The mustangs
stand close.
This keeps them warm.

canyon

The mustangs move to a canyon.
The canyon blocks the cold wind.

Mustangs have hooves.
The hooves are hard and strong.
The hooves help the mustangs run fast.

hooves

People can ride mustangs.

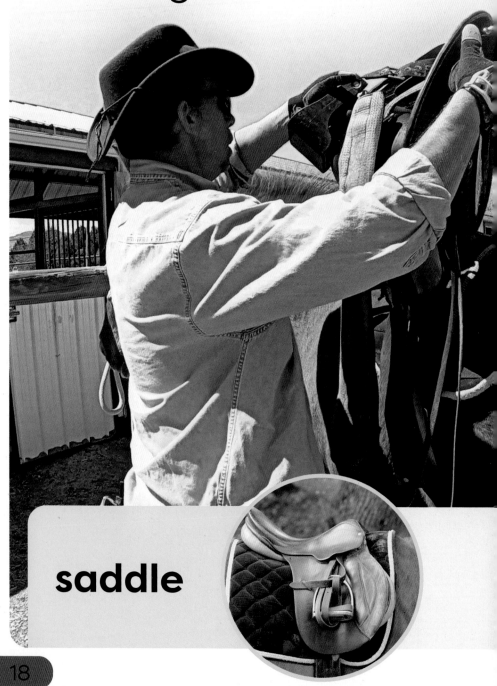

saddle

They put saddles on
the mustangs.
The mustangs help
the people go fast.

People share the mustangs' home. People build houses

run

on the grassland.
They watch the
mustangs run.

The mustangs run
through the grass.
The foal runs
with the band.
They run free.

Glossary

family
a group of animals that are related

leader
one who is in charge

safe
protected from danger

share
to use something with others

shrub
a bush with woody stems

Quiz

Answer the questions to see what you have learned. Check your answers with an adult.

1. What is a family of mustangs called?

2. What do mustangs eat?

3. Why do mustangs stand close together in the winter?

4. Where do mustangs live?

5. What do mustangs' hooves help them do?

1. A band 2. Grass, weeds, and shrubs 3. To stay warm
4. The grassland 5. Run fast